MACKINTOSH
TEXTILE DESIGNS

MACKINTOSH
TEXTILE DESIGNS

❖

ROGER BILLCLIFFE

JOHN MURRAY

For Owen and Andrew

Frontispiece: Charles Rennie Mackintosh,
a camera study by E. O. Hoppé, 1922
(*courtesy of Mansell Collection, London*)

© Roger Billcliffe 1982

First published 1982
by John Murray (Publishers) Ltd
50 Albemarle Street, London W1X 4BD

Design by Ian Craig

Printed in Great Britain by
The Fakenham Press, Fakenham

British Library Cataloguing in Publication Data

Mackintosh, Charles Rennie
    Mackintosh textile designs.
    1. Mackintosh, Charles Rennie   2. Textile
    crafts
    I. Title   II. Billcliffe, Roger
    746'.092'4   NK8898.M/
    ISBN 0-7195-3965-X

CONTENTS

All designs listed below are by Charles Rennie Mackintosh except those marked MM, Margaret Macdonald, or FM, Frances Macdonald.

All drawings are on white paper unless otherwise stated.
Dimensions are given in millimetres, height × width.
Items acknowledged to Glasgow University are in the Mackintosh Collection, Hunterian Art Gallery.

PREFACE

The names of many of the best British designers of the last hundred years or so are kept in the public eye through the continuing production of their designs for textiles. William Morris and C. F. A. Voysey, for instance, had considerable success in their lifetimes as fabric designers and many of their designs are still available today. One of the reasons that Mackintosh's work with textiles is so little known is that none of his fabrics can now be bought; indeed, I doubt whether any of them remained in production beyond the mid-1920s. Fortunately, a large group of Mackintosh's original drawings for textiles have survived in the private collections of James Meldrum and Sir Harry and Lady Barnes (these now transferred, respectively, to the Victoria and Albert Museum and the British Museum) and in the Mackintosh Estate at Glasgow University.

All of these designs were produced during the years Mackintosh was living in London, 1915-23. It is a period of his life about which we still know relatively little but, although he had few architectural commissions, Mackintosh maintained a fair output of watercolours and designs for furniture and fabrics. This book consists of a selection of the latter, showing the wide range of designs he made, many of them anticipating by as much as ten years the major decorative style of the 1920s — art deco.

I am grateful to Sir Harry Barnes and James Meldrum for access to their collections. The majority of drawings are now in the Hunterian Art Gallery at Glasgow University and I have to thank Pamela Reekie, Christopher Allan and Martin Hopkinson for arranging for the photography of so many of the items in their care. Finally, I must record my gratitude to Mary Newbery Sturrock for so willingly talking to me about her memories of Mackintosh during his Chelsea years. In the ten years that I have known her she has always made time to talk about Mackintosh. Her contact with him in Walberswick and London from 1914 to 1918 has given me many insights into his working methods. Everyone who has written on Mackintosh from Sir Nikolaus Pevsner and Thomas Howarth onwards knows how indefatigable her support of Mackintosh has been and how entertaining and enlightening it is to spend an hour or two in her company.

Roger Billcliffe
Glasgow, January 1982

MACKINTOSH AS A TEXTILE DESIGNER

In September 1906 Charles Rennie Mackintosh was authorised by the Governors of the Glasgow School of Art to prepare plans for the second phase of the School's new building. During the next twelve months Mackintosh produced a building which has been hailed as his masterpiece, a building which was to influence the course of twentieth-century architecture and design and which is now recognised world-wide as one of the great architectural achievements of the century. One might have expected its creator, not yet forty years old, to be a successful and sought-after designer with a busy office and clients queuing at his drawing board. Sadly, this is far from the truth for Mackintosh had had no major commissions since 1904 and none was forthcoming after the Glasgow School of Art was completed. Were it not for the support of his old friend, Catherine Cranston, who commissioned interiors in 1909 for her own home, Hous'hill, and in 1910–11 for one of her Tea Rooms, Mackintosh would have brought in virtually no work to his firm, Honeyman Keppie & Mackintosh.

It seems strange to reflect that while Mackintosh's progress was keenly followed in the German magazines *Dekorative Kunst* and *Deutsche Kunst und Dekoration*, Scottish and English periodicals virtually ignored him after his appearances in *The Studio* in 1896 and 1897. His success abroad at exhibitions in Vienna (1900), Turin (1902), Moscow (1903), Dresden (1904) and elsewhere was not echoed in Glasgow or London and he had remarkably few Scottish patrons – Walter Blackie, a publisher; William Davidson, a businessman; Fra Newbery, Headmaster of the School of Art; and Miss Cranston. Only the latter was able to consistently provide him with new work, and the commercially lucrative practice in domestic, commercial and public commissions which should have followed the success of The Hill House, Helensburgh, and the Glasgow School of Art eluded Mackintosh. This is not to say that his firm was unsuccessful; indeed, without the work brought in by his partner, John Keppie, Mackintosh would have had a very lean time, even during the years 1900 to 1905 when he was personally very busy. Needless to say, this disparate distribution of achievement within the firm caused Mackintosh and his partner some concern. Although Mackintosh, without doubt, assisted Keppie with several of his designs during this period, he was not bringing in the new jobs to keep both himself and his own draughtsmen employed.

Depressed and rejected, Mackintosh's performance within the firm worsened. Melancholia led to a gradual dependence on alcohol and matters came to a head over some uncompleted design for a local competition with which Mackintosh had been entrusted. By mutual agreement Mackintosh and Keppie dissolved their partnership in 1913 and Mackintosh set up in practice on his own. He had no greater success alone, however, and in 1914, with his wife Margaret, he set out for a recuperative holiday in Walberswick.

The Newberys had had a studio-cottage for some years in this coastal Suffolk village and it was doubtless at their suggestion that the Mackintoshes took lodgings there. Fra Newbery's daughter, Mary Sturrock, believes that Mackintosh's visit to Walberswick was merely a holiday, an opportunity away from Glasgow to consider his position. The house at 78 Southpark Avenue in Glasgow was not sold and the MacNairs, Margaret's sister and brother-in-law, lived there for a while. In fact, Mackintosh did not sell the house until about 1919, when it was bought by William Davidson, and so the possibility of returning to Glasgow was always available to him.

One of the options apparently open to Mackintosh was to move to Vienna and set up practice there. His correspondence with German and Austrian friends was, in 1915, to lead to local suspicion that he was a spy. What was discussed in the letters is not known but the outbreak of war in 1914 put paid to any thoughts of moving to Austria. It also suspended the arrangement Mackintosh had with a German publisher for a book of botanical drawings on which he had started work in Walberswick in 1914. What had started out as a holiday gradually grew into a more settled sojourn. The Newberys returned to Glasgow at the end of the summer but the Mackintoshes remained there for another year. The 'espionage' episode, when Mackintosh came under suspicion as a German spy, caused them to leave Walberswick and move to London where Mackintosh resolved to build up a new practice as an architect and designer.

They took lodgings in Chelsea and rented two studios at 43A Glebe Place. Financially, they were not well off. Under the terms of his partnership agreement Mackintosh was to receive a percentage of the fees for a period of three years after leaving the practice and Margaret had a small private income of her own. The war, however, placed new obstacles in Mackintosh's path. New building was severely restricted and thus the opportunities open to him were dramatically reduced. He had one stroke of luck; a commission from W. J. Bassett-Lowke for the remodelling of a terrace house, 78 Derngate, in Northampton, but when it was published in *Ideal Home* in August 1920 Mackintosh was not mentioned and no new work came from it.

To supplement his income from the Bassett-Lowke commissions, which continued spasmodically through to 1919, Mackintosh began to paint watercolours which he sent to various exhibitions in the hope of making some sales. *Peonies*, *Anemones*, *Yellow Tulips* and *Grey Iris* are some of his most beautiful watercolours, all produced during his stay in London from 1915 to 1923, but none of them was sold. Whether he also tried to sell furniture designs to manufacturers such as Heal's we do not know. Heal's certainly made some of the furniture he designed for Bassett-Lowke but Mackintosh had not designed furniture on a commercial basis since the few pieces commissioned by Guthrie & Wells in Glasgow in the mid-1890s.

Since that time all of Mackintosh's design work had come about as a result of some architectural commission. The furniture and metalwork were all related to specific rooms and he was not used to designing for a more general market. This being the case, it seems strange that the one venture he undertook in London in order to provide some form of income was the design of fabrics for two textile firms, Foxton's and Sefton's. What makes this move even more unexpected is that Mackintosh had never before designed printed fabrics, most curtains and upholstery in his Glasgow work being either stencilled or embroidered in appliqué. Much of this earlier work had been done in collaboration with his wife, Mackintosh providing the design and Margaret the execution, but there is evidence in these new designs of a much closer working relationship between the two artists.

Mrs Sturrock believes that it was Claud Lovat Fraser, who came to know the couple well during their stay in Chelsea, who introduced Mackintosh to the two leading textile producers, Foxton's and Sefton's. We do not know whether he worked for other manufacturers and only these two names ever appear on any of the surviving drawings. Little is known of the contractual relationship between them and Mackintosh but he seems to have worked on a freelance basis, receiving between £5 and £20 for each design. The only year for which any record survives is 1920, and notes in Mackintosh's diary show that he received about £200 in fees from the two firms. Unfortunately their records have all been destroyed; William Foxton wrote to Thomas Howarth in 1945 reporting that all his papers and samples had been destroyed in an air raid in 1942. What little remains of the two firms' output is now in the Victoria and Albert Museum; there are many samples of the Registered Designs acquired from the Manchester Registration Office by Elizabeth Aslin for the Circulation Department in the early 1950s. Of these hundreds of samples, however, only two can reasonably be identified as being designed by Mackintosh (see Plate 67).

The floral patterns of the wall stencils and curtains at The Hill House were not to form the basis of this new group of designs. The spare, linear motifs of roses and tendrils were replaced by more aggressive patterns, densely crowded on to the paper with none of the meaningful empty spaces which characterise the early stencils. The only parallel between these Chelsea drawings and any Glasgow work can be seen in one of Mackintosh's last rooms for Miss Cranston, the Cloister Room at Ingram Street of 1911. His use of green, blue and red diapers connected together in long strings and outlined in black can be seen in many of the Chelsea designs. The Cloister Room, and to a certain extent the Library of the Glasgow School of Art, can be seen as experiments in a new decorative style which were not fulfilled in Glasgow. The move to London seemed to act as a catalyst for Mackintosh and in his work at 78 Derngate, Northampton, and in his textile designs Mackintosh developed a wholly new vocabulary based on his later Glasgow work.

Although these designs for fabrics are rare examples of Mackintosh breaking with his practice of designing only for specific projects over which he had total control there is no doubt that he had specific interiors and furniture in mind for many of these fabrics. From 1915 to 1919 Mackintosh worked on 78 Derngate and Candida Cottage for W. J. Bassett-Lowke. In these two houses, and in other jobs for Bassett-Lowke's friends, Mackintosh created the kind of interiors which suited perfectly the new range of abstract-patterned fabrics which he was designing. The hall-parlour at Derngate with its black ceiling and walls – the latter covered with a stencilled pattern of overlapping triangles in green, blue, yellow, grey and white – had curtains with a design very close to the diaper pattern of the Cloister Room. A variant of the tulip pattern (Plate 23) was used in a washstand and in a panel behind the beds in a bedroom designed for Sidney Horstmann, a business colleague of Bassett-Lowke, in a house at Bath. These rooms had each very individual characters – the hall at Derngate a daring composition in black with sculptural furniture and a deliberate use of the lattice and triangle as decorative motifs; while Horstmann's bedroom had simple furniture, boxy and unpretentious, with inlays of aluminium and mother-of-pearl. Obviously, Mackintosh could not always rely on the purchasers of his fabric using it in the same way, but this does give us an indication of the types of interiors in which he hoped to see it used.

It is difficult, if not impossible, to construct a chronology for the 120 or so designs which now survive. Mackintosh appears to have received his first commissions about 1915 and was certainly producing designs in some quantity in 1920. In 1923 he and Margaret left London for France and at that date, if not before, he terminated his arrangement with the manufacturers. Hardly any of the designs are dated and the simple notes on some of the mounts are no help in dating them. I think it is possible, however, to classify a few as early, that is dating from 1915 or thereabouts, and several others can be dated to c. 1917 because of their relationship to decorations produced for Miss Cranston's last venture in Glasgow, the Dug-Out. This was a tea room which set out to evoke the atmosphere of the trenches for those left at home in Glasgow – more salubrious trenches were never seen in the battlefields of France and Belgium.

The earlier designs all seem to be based on simple stylisations of flowers or bouquets. Mackintosh realised that his delicate drawings of wild flowers could not be transformed into flat, repetitive patterns but this early group of designs are all based on fairly free watercolours of bouquets of cut flowers. This change from wild to cultivated flowers – roses, chrysanthemums, peonies and tulips – is reflected in

Mackintosh's paintings of 1916–18. These designs seem hesitant, with some uncertainty about pattern repeats both horizontally and vertically, and it may be that some of them, particularly the more formal bouquets, may have been intended as simple printed panels for use as cushion covers or similar articles.

The highly finished watercolours of cut flowers in vases also give us some clue to the date of a few of the fabrics. *Blue garlands* (Plate 43) can be seen in the background of *Begonias*, a watercolour dated 1916; a yellow and black geometric pattern is reflected in a mirror in *Anemones*, also *c*. 1916; bold zigzag patterns and overlapping waves appear in *White Roses* (1920) and *Peonies* (*c*. 1919) respectively. All of this is fairly negative evidence, however, and merely serves to confirm my belief that Mackintosh was able to vary rapidly the format of these designs, possibly at the request of the manufacturers. Unlike the eight years in Glasgow from 1897 to 1905, when Mackintosh was working at a hectic pace, the work produced in these eight years in London, 1915 to 1923, cannot be so easily categorised on grounds of style and content.

Three other groups of designs can also be related to other projects. Motifs from the two painted panels, *The Little Hills* (Plates 51/52), reappear in a number of designs based on stylised daisies. According to Mrs Sturrock *The Little Hills* were entirely Margaret's work and they were painted for the Dug-Out about 1917. The subject matter, cherubs and butterflies, is certainly typical of Margaret and the composition is reminiscent of *The Opera of the Sea* and *The Opera of the Winds*, two small gesso panels which Margaret made in 1903 for a piano which Mackintosh designed for Fritz Wärndorfer of Vienna. The daisy motif, however, I believe to be Mackintosh's invention and I think he was also responsible for the details of the 'landscape' in the two panels, at least in design if not execution. The ranks of tulip shapes supporting the four upper cherubs also suggests the hand of an architect and they are certainly most unlike any other motifs from Margaret's earlier work. (A drawing relating to these tulips, almost certainly in Mackintosh's hand, is in the Victoria and Albert Museum.)

The daisy-chain patterns, in purple, black, blue, green and yellow, are some of Mackintosh's most elegant fabric designs. They form part of the group of designs based on stylised flowers and a second group of designs can also be shown to have links with one of Margaret's paintings. Margaret reworked her gesso panel *The Opera of the Sea* into a large painting (collection: Hessisches Landesmuseum, Darmstadt). As with *The Little Hills*, the execution is almost certainly Margaret's, as is the overall composition. Several details, however, reappear in some of the most colourful of Mackintosh's textile designs. All of these are based on a motif of stylised tobacco flowers and one drawing exists (Plate 7) which is a direct tracing, reversed, from the hair of one of the figures in the large *Opera of the Sea*. Mackintosh developed the design in a spectacular way and in one of the best of the surviving drawings

(Plate 9) we can see how, while keeping the basic motif, Mackintosh has subtly changed the framework of the drawing to produce a more satisfactory design for a patterned fabric. This drawing also shows how the character of the design can be changed dramatically by altering or reversing the colourways or varying the background colour and texture.

We do not know why Margaret painted this large version of *The Opera of the Sea*. It was a large picture (1440 × 1600 mm) and it seems unlikely that it was a speculative piece of work. *The Little Hills*, although supposedly painted for the Dug-Out, found its way into the Macdonald family collection, as did *The Opera of the Sea*. Neither of the works, however, is listed in the inventory of Margaret's estate drawn up in 1933. Was *The Opera of the Sea* also a Dug-Out panel? On subject matter alone this seems unlikely but the question is complicated by the recent re-appearance of two similarly sized pictures, making one panel, in the collection of the Glasgow School of Art (Plates 46 and 47).

Undoubtedly in Mackintosh's hand these two paintings date from the Chelsea period and incorporate numerous passages that can be related to a third group of designs for textiles. These fabric designs are here used as background pattern – in-fill – for an elaborate composition parallelling stylised human and stylised plant forms, an updating of his stencil wall decorations for the Buchanan Street Tea Rooms of 1896. Were these two pictures also intended for the Dug-Out? If so, where were they located and how did they become separated from *The Little Hills* and *The Opera of the Sea* which became the property of the Macdonald family before 1933? These are questions which cannot be answered here, but the appearance of motifs from the textiles in these three compositions show quite clearly that Mackintosh was not producing the designs in a vacuum. Speculative and commercial they may have been, but they are not as far outside the mainstream of his development as a designer as has been previously suggested.

Mackintosh used stylised plant forms on several other designs for textiles. Roses, chrysanthemums, sprouting corms and bulbs were all abstracted to produce a repetitive pattern suitable for use in long lengths of fabric. Organic motifs form the largest group of designs but perhaps the most exciting of the remaining drawings is the series of abstract patterns based on geometric shapes. Triangles, grids, squares and diamonds in vivid colours of yellow, blue, green and purple, often set against grey or black backgrounds, show that Mackintosh had lost none of the ingenuity and power of invention that is to be seen in his earlier Glasgow work. These are 'Jazz Age' designs, several years before their time, and they must have looked stunning when made into curtains, or used as dress or upholstery materials.

Sadly, just a few of these fabrics survive and we can know them only from the drawings. These hint at the type of fabric to be used – some were for chiffon, silk and voile, others are noted as 'furniture fabric' – but the texture of the material is rarely noted by Mackintosh. Occasionally a drawing will have a colour key showing the printer how the colourways might be changed to alter the visual effect but otherwise Mackintosh gives very little information on the drawings. Apart from the uses noted at 78 Derngate and in the bedroom at Bath we have no knowledge of how he intended the fabrics to be used, nor do we know how many of the surviving designs were actually put into production.

In contrast with his designs for the Glasgow furniture and interiors, about which we have a great deal of information, there is very little documentary evidence to indicate the range of work that Mackintosh produced in Chelsea or to show how these designs were received. We can speculate that Foxton's and Sefton's were pleased with the designs; £200 for designs in a single year was, after all, a reasonable sum of money. We can also speculate that Mackintosh was not content to carry on producing them if he could not at the same time practise as an architect. However successful his textile designs were they obviously did not soften the disappointment he suffered from the rejection of his architectural designs. In the early 1920s Allan Ure, a young Glaswegian architect at that time working as a draughtsman in the London office of Burnet & Tait, visited Mackintosh in Chelsea and found him morose and obviously depressed by the treatment he had received over his designs for the studios and flats in Glebe Place and off Cheyne Walk. Ure knew Mackintosh's Glasgow work and hoped to find a job in Mackintosh's office. No job and no office existed, however, and shortly afterwards Mackintosh turned his back on architects and architecture and left London for the south of France and a new career as a watercolour painter.

The textile designs, however, give no clue to Mackintosh's depression and rejection. As a body of work they are consistently brilliant in their range of decorative form and colour and the mastery of an area of design that was totally new to their creator. After he left Glasgow Mackintosh was dogged with disappointment and straightforward bad luck. His Chelsea years have been ignored as a backwater of his career but Mackintosh came to London full of hope for the future. He worked hard and produced a creditable group of designs for interiors and furniture – over fifty pieces of furniture for Bassett-Lowke alone – as well as one of his most brilliant rooms – the 1919 guest bedroom at 78 Derngate, Northampton. The Chelsea Studios and the Theatre for Margaret Morris would have been exciting designs and would surely have led to a very different practice from that which he had left behind in Glasgow. The textile designs fitted perfectly into this new career but, sadly, they were the only part of it which was fully realised. Just as Mackintosh could not remain in Glasgow solely as an interior designer for Miss Cranston, nor could he stomach a future as a graphic designer while lesser architects received the commissions he had hoped would be his.

These designs, and the series of watercolours he produced after 1915 until his death in 1928, are the success stories from what was otherwise a tragic period in the life of one of Britain's greatest architects. Glasgow, the second city of the Empire, had rejected him; the first city offered him little more. Although Mackintosh treated every job that came to him with the same seriousness — spoons, chairs, beds, houses, schools and cathedrals were all important to him — he must have felt some anger at the relative success of his fabrics against the failure of his equally powerful architectural designs.

Mackintosh's solution to his dilemma was to sacrifice both and after 1923 he designed neither fabrics nor buildings. Had some of the actual fabrics survived our attitude to much of Mackintosh's later work might have been very different, for in these drawings we can see that same breadth of imagination, the same flair and inventive qualities that characterise his furniture and other graphic designs. Above all, his skill as a draughtsman and instinctive sense of colour is revealed as having lost none of the power shown in his work of twenty years earlier.

1 Chrysanthemum   *Watercolour 257 × 235*   Glasgow University

Virtually a finished picture in its own right this very formalised flower may have been intended for a large repeat fabric

18

3 Stylised rose   *Pencil and watercolour 188 × 219*   Glasgow University

A variation on *Chrysanthemum* showing a repeat pattern from a single flower motif

2 (*opposite*) Roses on a chequered ground   *Watercolour and pencil 1015 × 557*
Glasgow University

This is the only surviving design to have an inscription with an address in Walberswick.
Mackintosh was living in this East Anglian village during 1914 and 1915, which makes this
drawing one of the earliest known designs. It is possible, however, that this is a design for a wall
decoration, presumably stencilled, as the scale of the whole design and the individual elements are
much larger than any of the subsequent textile designs produced in Chelsea

4 Basket of flowers *Watercolour 317 × 300* Glasgow University

5 Bouquet *Watercolour and gouache 414 × 337* Glasgow University

Mackintosh has cut out the panel of flowers and stuck it on a black background. It seems as if he was making some attempt to make a repeat pattern from the design but the overall effect is very fussy and unresolved

6 Stylised dahlias *Pencil and watercolour 203 × 125* Glasgow University

Although this drawing is more like a finished watercolour than a fabric design it was later traced by Mackintosh and used as part of a repeating pattern

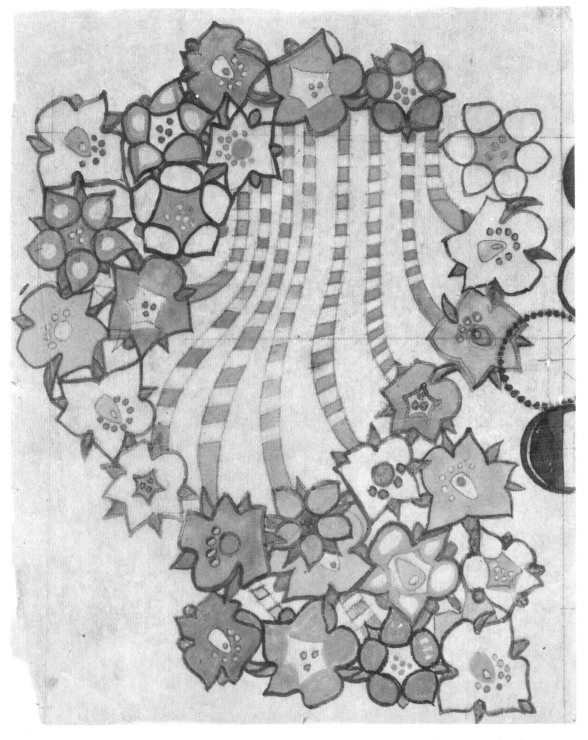

7 Pink tobacco flower   *Pencil and watercolour on tracing paper 257 × 265*   Glasgow University

The drawing is a reversed tracing from the hair of a figure in *The Opera of the Sea* (Hessisches Landesmuseum, Darmstadt; reproduced in colour in Mario Amaya, *Art Nouveau*, 1966, p. 50). The panel is certainly the work of Margaret Macdonald Mackintosh and is a reworking of a gesso panel by her of 1903, which was fitted into a piano designed by her husband for Fritz Wärndorfer. Mackintosh may have collaborated with his wife on this painting, particularly on the faces and this floral headdress which are painted on 'papier-collé'. This tracing is certainly in his hand and a number of finished designs for textiles were developed from it

24

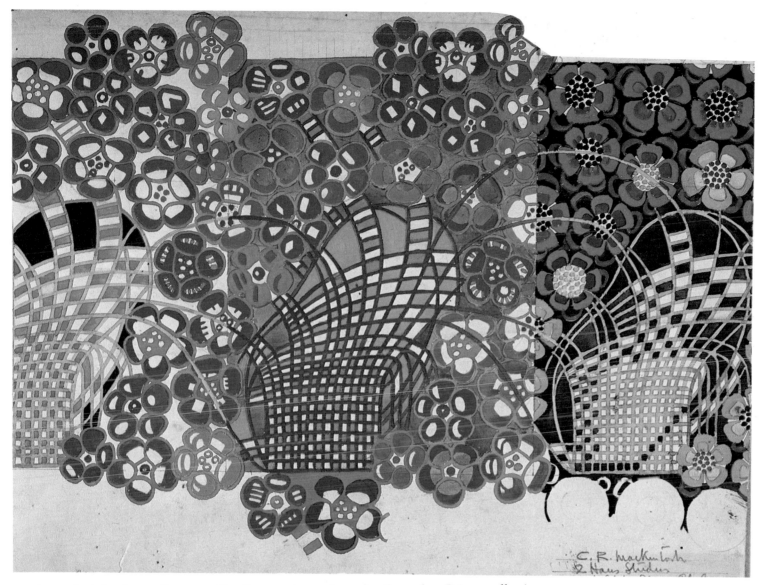

9 Blue and pink tobacco flowers   *Pencil, watercolour and gouache 560 × 365*   Private collection

This design is developed from the tracing from *The Opera of the Sea* (Pl. 7). It has a design repeat of 200 × 152 and Mackintosh has shown it in three different colourways

8 (*opposite*) Tobacco flower   *Watercolour and gouache 262 × 210*   Glasgow University

Although there is still the hint of a finished picture about this design the elements of a repetitive overall pattern are more apparent

10 Stylised flowers on a trellis   *Pencil and watercolour on tracing paper 301 × 238*
Victoria and Albert Museum

11 Tobacco flowers and fruit *Pencil on tracing paper 464 × 317* Victoria and Albert Museum

This drawing shows how Mackintosh built up the basic structure of his designs, here using tracing paper to take various elements from existing designs to make a new pattern

28

12 (*opposite*) Stylised chrysanthemums
Pencil and watercolour 480 × 550
Glasgow University

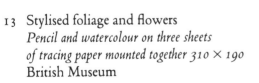

13 Stylised foliage and flowers
*Pencil and watercolour on three sheets
of tracing paper mounted together 310 × 190*
British Museum

Whether experimenting for his own sake,
or providing finished alternatives for the
manufacturer, Mackintosh shows here
how bold changes in colour can
completely alter the character of a design

14 Stylised flowers – purple and pink
Pencil and watercolour on tracing paper
360 × 273   Glasgow University

15 Stylised foliage and flowers
Pencil and watercolour on tracing paper
240 × 190   British Museum

A preparatory version of No. 13

16 Stylised chrysanthemums *Pencil and watercolour 292 × 209* Glasgow University

17 Sprouting corms   *Pencil and watercolour 180 × 165*   Glasgow University

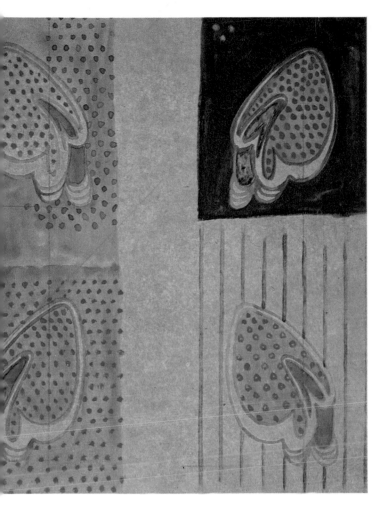

19 Strawberries
Pencil and watercolour on tracing paper 216 × 185
Glasgow University

18 Flowering bulb
Pencil and watercolour on tracing paper 276 × 220
Glasgow University

Bulbs and corms had been favourite motifs in the watercolours of Mackintosh and the Macdonald sisters in the 1890s. Here he returns to the theme, formalising even further the shape of the bulb to produce a decorative pattern

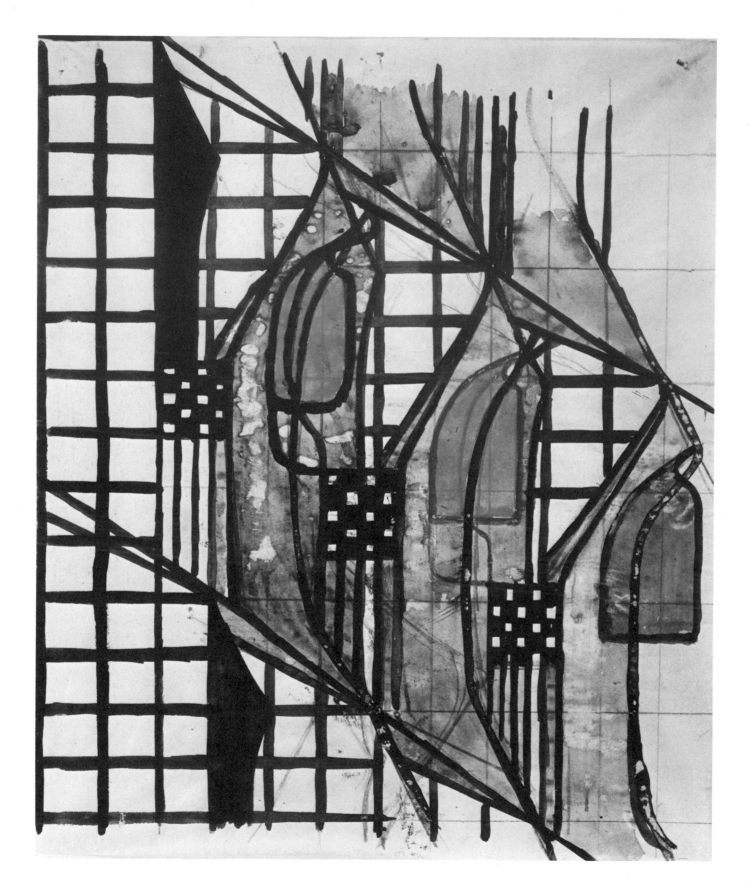

21 Rose and teardrop *Pencil and watercolour 216 × 238* Glasgow University

Based on a tracing of No. 22, Mackintosh has altered the number of roses in the design but the repeat does not seem to work out correctly. He also seems to have experimented with the colour of the roses, substituting a grey-purple for the pinks of No. 22; and the black outlines have here been replaced by green

20 (*opposite*) Tulip and lattice – diagonal *Pencil and watercolour 245 × 204* British Museum

22 Rose and teardrop   *Pencil and watercolour 255 × 255*
Glasgow University

Mackintosh had stylised roses from an early point in his
career but this design is probably the most elaborate
rendering of the theme. Each of the twenty roses is
different – a game which Mackintosh enjoyed playing
and which is seen at its best in the carved pendant panels
around the gallery in the Library at Glasgow School of Art

23 (*opposite*) Tulip and lattice   *Pencil and watercolour*
397 × 288   Glasgow University

One of the most complete of the surviving drawings, this
design shows how Mackintosh amalgamated organic
and geometric motifs into a single pattern. The
latticework, with its varying sizes of squares, echoes the
astragals of the windows in the scheme for studios in
Glebe Place and Cheyne Walk, Chelsea, in 1920

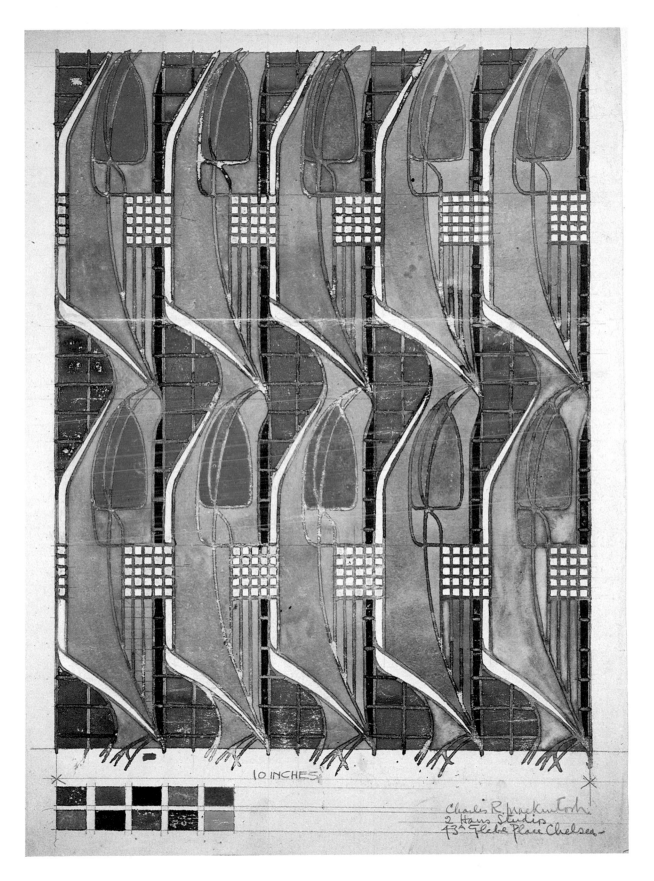

10 INCHES

Charles R. Mackintosh
2 Hans Studio
43ª Glebe Place Chelsea

24 Stylised tulips on a chequered ground
Pencil and watercolour on tracing paper 230 × 102
Glasgow University

By superimposing the tulip motif from Nos. 25–7
on a chequered background Mackintosh has
disguised the organic origins of the design

25 (*opposite*) Stylised tulips   *Pencil and watercolour on
tracing paper 394 × 284*   Glasgow University

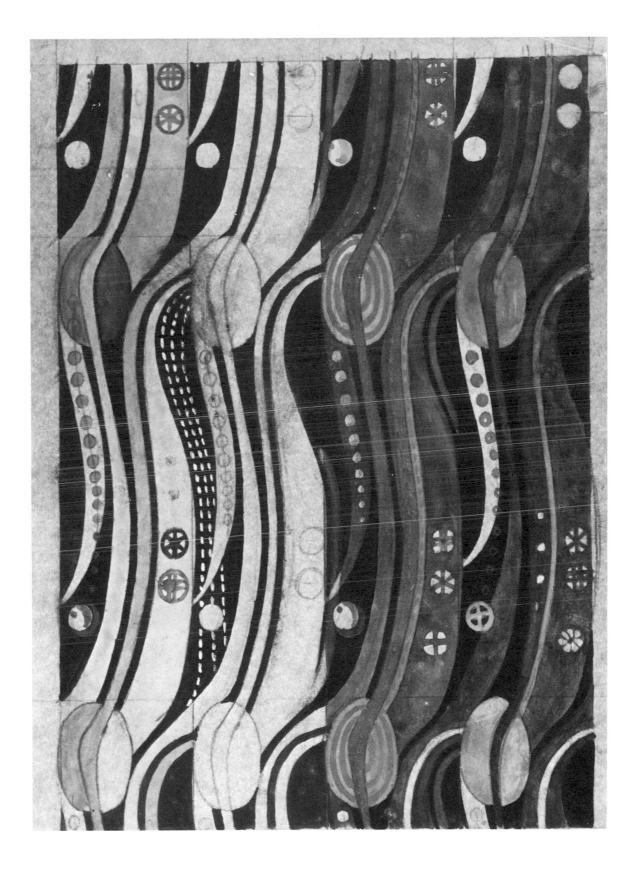

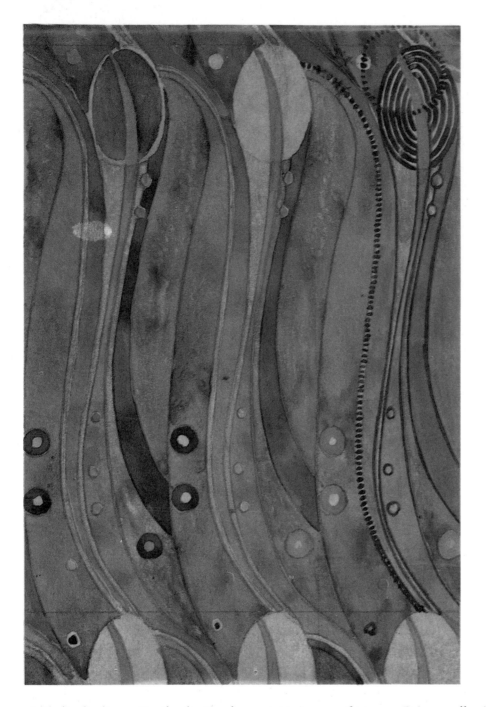

26 Stylised tulips   *Pencil and watercolour on tracing paper 298 × 217*   Private collection

Another variation on the tulip form which appears in several textile designs
and also in at least two of his watercolour paintings of this period. The
abstraction of the shape allows other interpretations of its origin: is it a
sprouting seed or even a tadpole? We know that Mackintosh had been
fascinated by the biological specimens he had been shown when he had
designed the Queen Margaret Medical College, Glasgow, in 1895; are some
of these shapes recollections of the tiny animals he had seen in the microscope?
A note on the mount indicates that this design was intended for use on silk

27 Stylised tulip
*Pencil and watercolour
on tracing paper 252 × 168*
Glasgow University

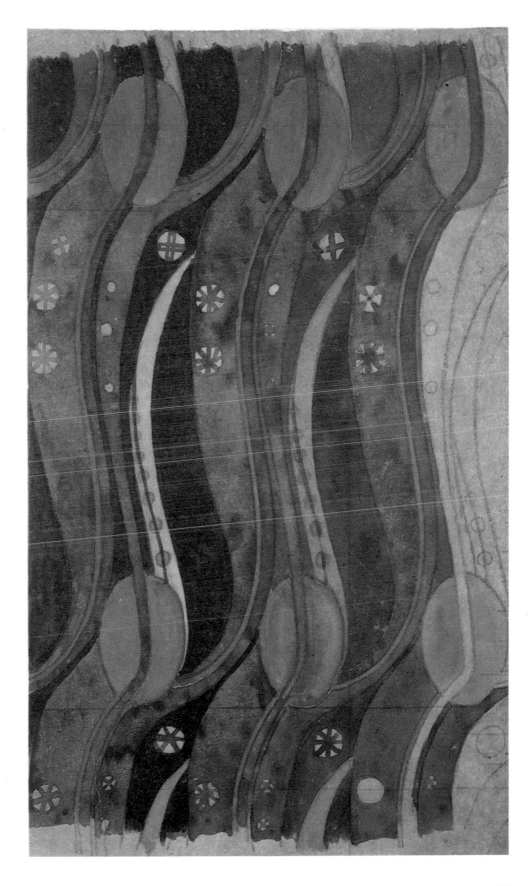

28   Margaret and Frances Macdonald   Vanity handkerchief *c.* 1898
Pencil and watercolour 334 × 326   Glasgow University

The peacock was a favourite *fin-de-siècle* motif not only with the Glasgow
designers but also with many of the Aesthetic Movement and Arts and Crafts
designers. Mackintosh used it on a large scale at the Buchanan Street Tea Rooms
in 1896 and the Macdonald sisters used it here in a much more delicate manner
on this rather strange circular handkerchief

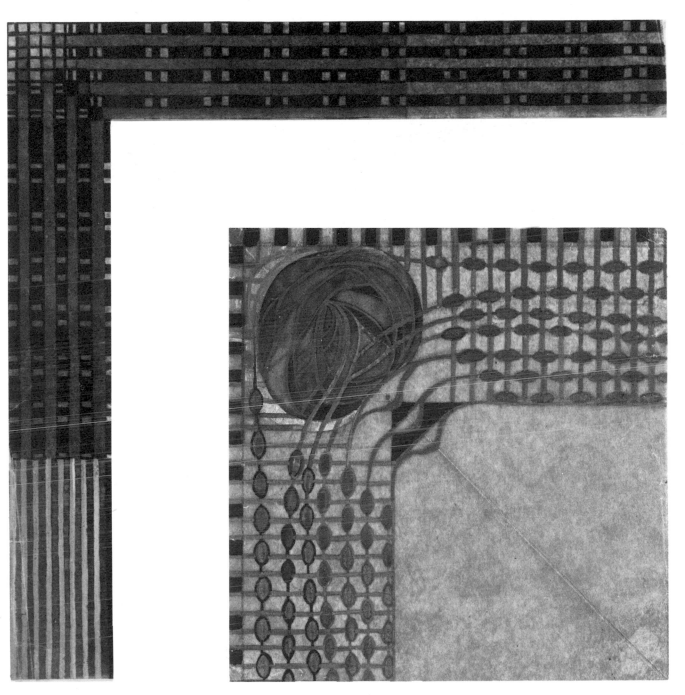

29 (*outer*) Margaret Macdonald Mackintosh   Border for a handkerchief   *Pen and ink, pencil and watercolour 262 × 262 (× 40 wide)*   Glasgow University

A full-size drawing of a quarter of the finished design showing four colourways. The design was bought by Foxton's

30 (*inner*) Border pattern – stylised rose   *Watercolour on tracing paper 133 × 133*   Victoria and Albert Museum

Possibly another design for a handkerchief, this time by Mackintosh

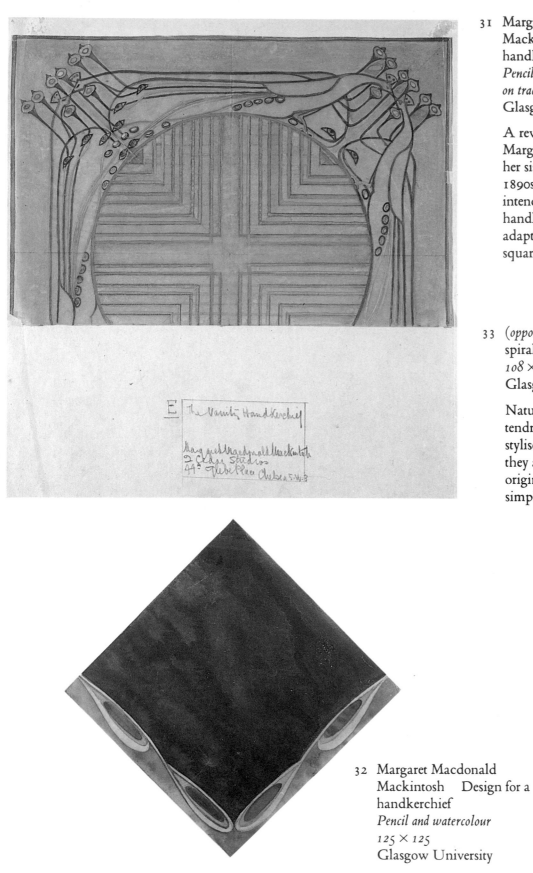

31 Margaret Macdonald
Mackintosh Vanity
handkerchief *c.* 1920
*Pencil and watercolour
on tracing paper 160 × 252*
Glasgow University

A reworking of a design
Margaret had produced with
her sister Frances in the late
1890s. The earlier design was
intended for a circular
handkerchief but she has now
adapted it for the more usual
square of cloth

33 (*opposite*) Orange and purple
spirals *Pencil and watercolour
108 × 141*
Glasgow University

Natural forms of stems and
tendrils have here been
stylised to the point where
they almost lose their organic
origins and can be seen quite
simply as abstract patterns

32 Margaret Macdonald
Mackintosh Design for a
handkerchief
*Pencil and watercolour
125 × 125*
Glasgow University

45

34 Spirals and squares
Pencil and watercolour 376 × 170
Glasgow University

35 Triangles and squares
Pencil and watercolour 248 × 202
Glasgow University

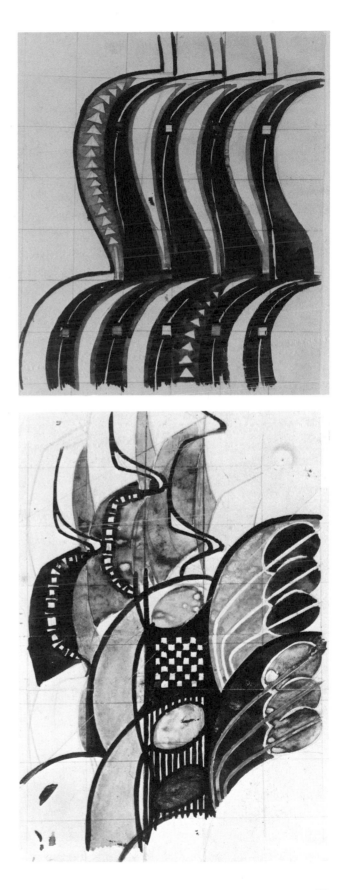

36 Tulips and checks
Pencil and watercolour 255 × 204
Glasgow University

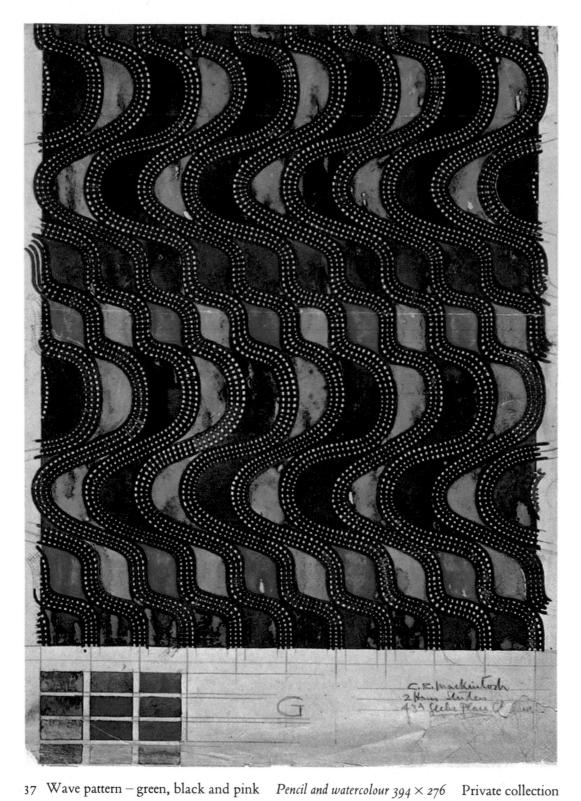

37 Wave pattern – green, black and pink   *Pencil and watercolour 394 × 276*   Private collection

One of the most accomplished drawings, bold in pattern and colour but with the subtleties of many of Mackintosh's designs. He has provided for four alternative colourways, exchanging the green and pink for shades of purple or yellow

38 (*opposite*) Hourglass pattern
Watercolour 254 × 203
Victoria and Albert Museum

39 Stylised flowers and chequerwork   *Pencil and watercolour 240 × 203*   Glasgow University

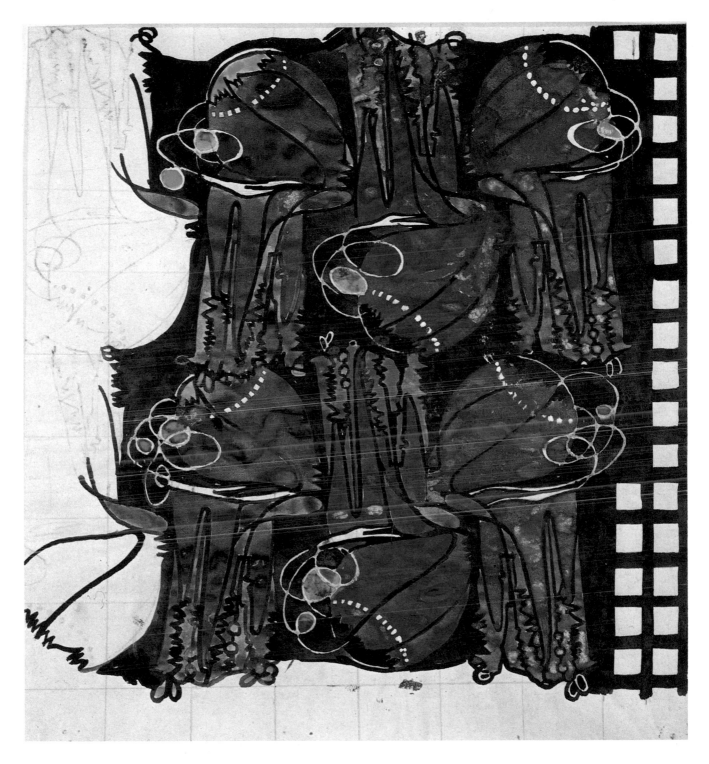

40 Stylised plant form – black, purple, green and pink   *Pencil and watercolour 228 × 203*
Glasgow University

Black is the dominant colour of a fine group of designs which amalgamate organic and geometric
forms. They were probably designs for voiles or dress fabrics and a number of them were bought
by Foxton's

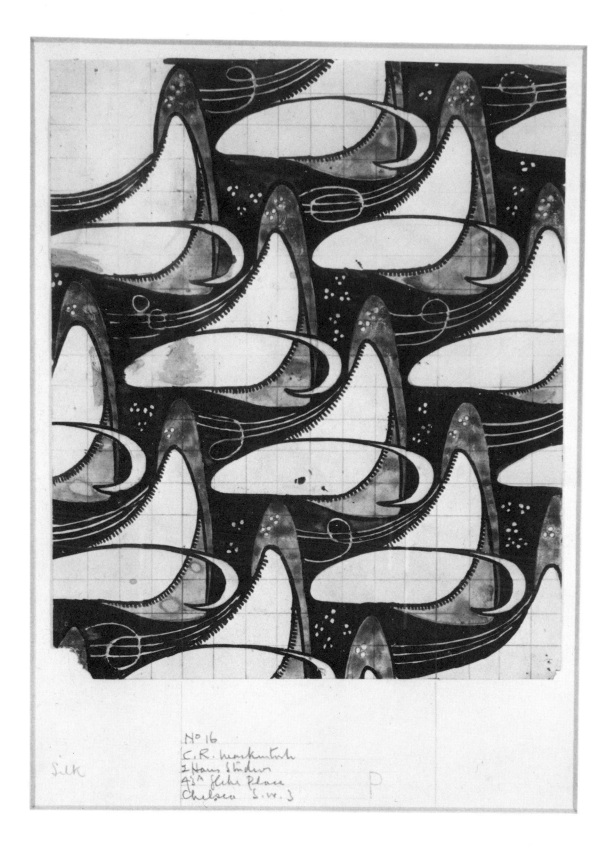

41 Design for silk *Pencil and watercolour on tracing paper 242 × 202* Private collection

42 Odalisque *Pencil and watercolour 202 × 127*
Glasgow University

This tongue-in-cheek nude disguised with stylised roses is possibly the only design where Mackintosh has used the human form as the basis of his repeating pattern. The reaction of the fabric manufacturer is not, unfortunately, known

43 Blue garlands   *Pencil and watercolour 240 × 190*
British Museum

45 (*opposite*) Rectangles and green checks
Pencil and watercolour 203 × 178
Glasgow University

44   Stylised daisies – purple, green and yellow
Pencil and watercolour on tracing paper 470 × 502
Glasgow University

One of the most elaborate and elegant of
Mackintosh's designs. Similarities between this
drawing and the hair of some of the figures in *The
Little Hills* suggest that Mackintosh may have had a
hand in the design of these paintings, if not their
execution

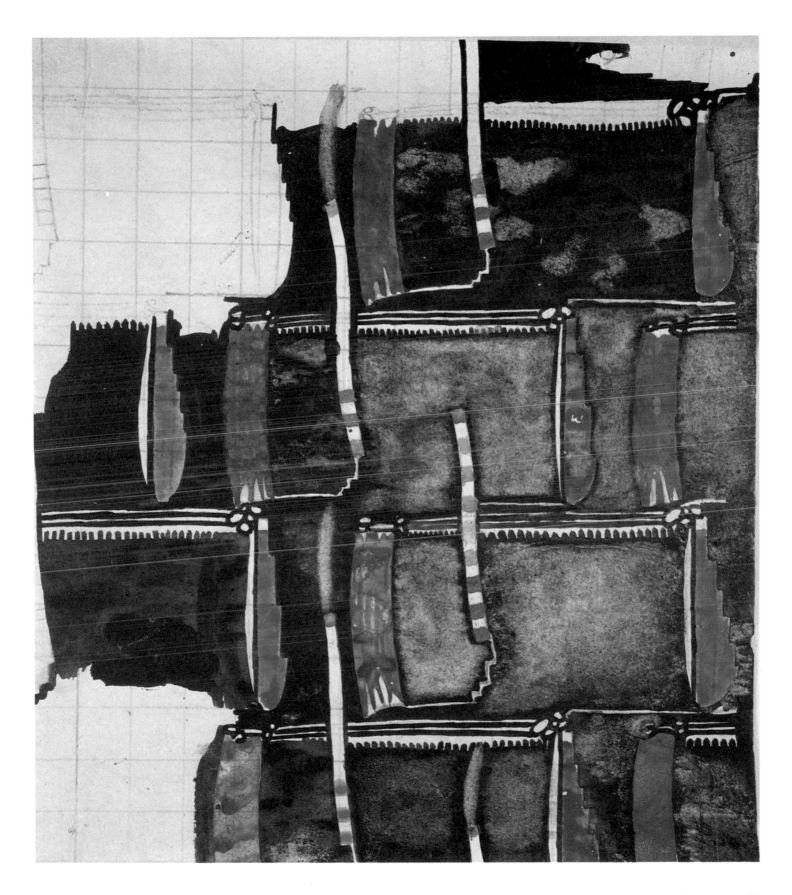

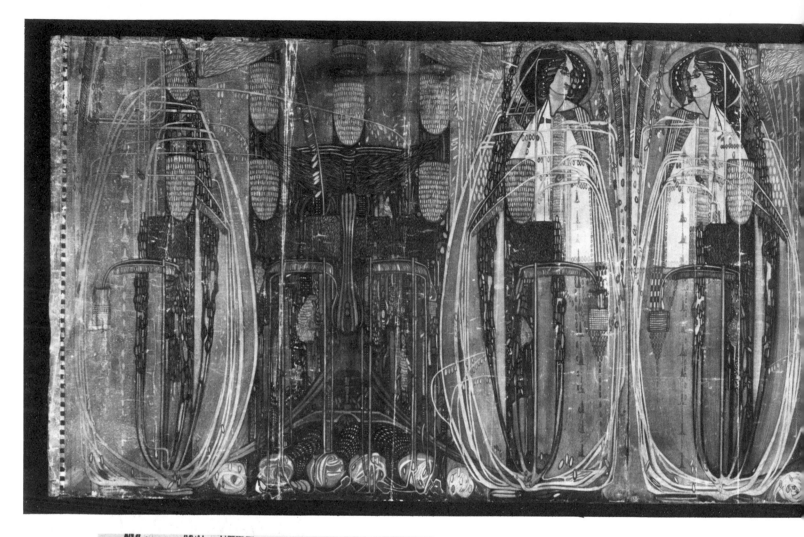

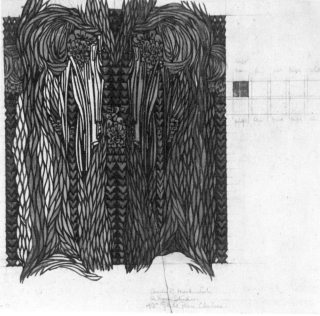

47 Stylised foliage – green and purple
Pen and ink, pencil and watercolour 355 × 400
Glasgow University

These swaying and intertwined stems of
grasses take on an almost human aspect
in this design. The background consists
of overlapping triangles – a motif used
extensively in the stencil decorations at 78
Derngate, Northampton, in 1915–16

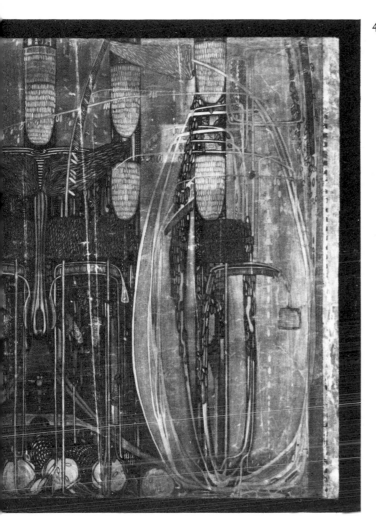

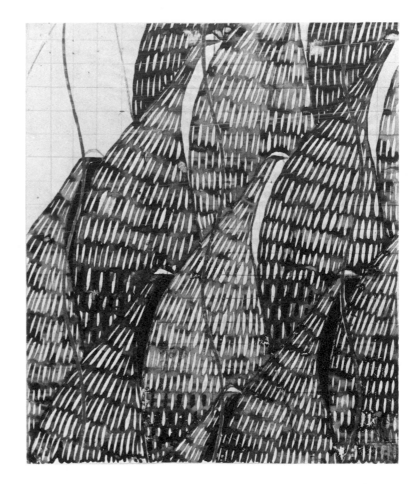

46 Figures and foliage
Oil on canvas, on two panels, 1370 × 1700 each
Glasgow School of Art

48 Furnishing fabric – purple and green
Pencil and watercolour 238 × 203
Glasgow University

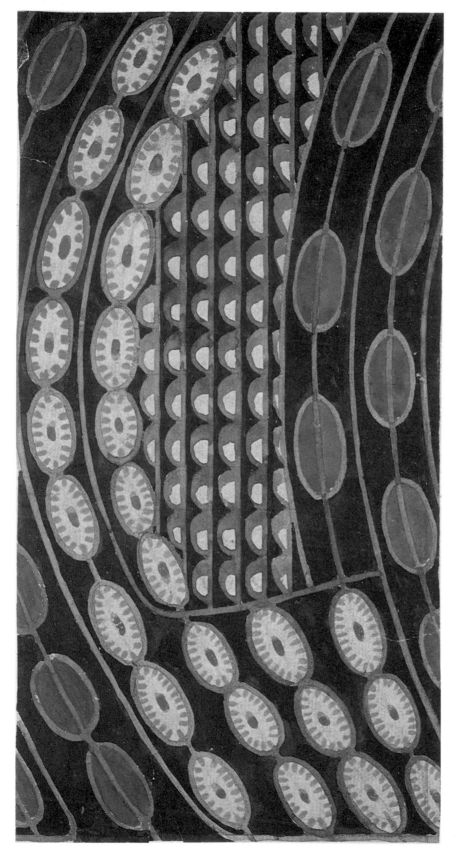

49 Stylised daisies – purple on black
Pencil and watercolour on tracing paper
235 × 121   Glasgow University

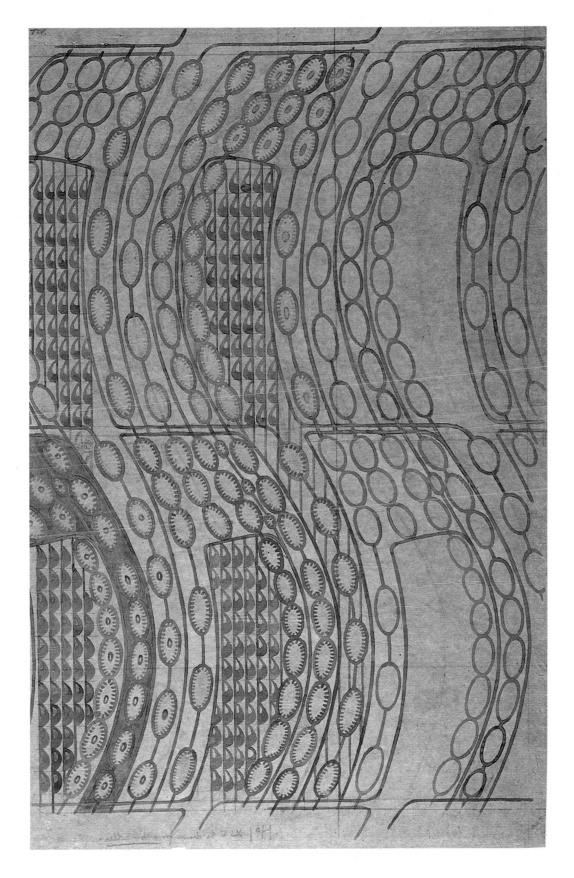

50 Stylised daisies – purple and blue   *Pencil and watercolour on tracing paper 510 × 323* Glasgow University

A group of designs using a stylised daisy seem to stem from a similar motif in the two paintings *The Little Hills* by Margaret Macdonald Mackintosh (Pl. 51/52). This design has instructions that it be redrawn for a 16-inch roller

51/52 Margaret Macdonald Mackintosh   The Little Hills   *Oil on canvas, two panels each*
1535 × 1510   Glasgow University

These panels were intended for use in the extension to Miss Cranston's Willow Tea Rooms – the Dug-Out. This topically named set of rooms was situated in a basement in Sauchiehall Street, Glasgow, and opened in 1917. They were Mackintosh's last commission in Glasgow and the only examples of his Northampton style to be seen in his home city.

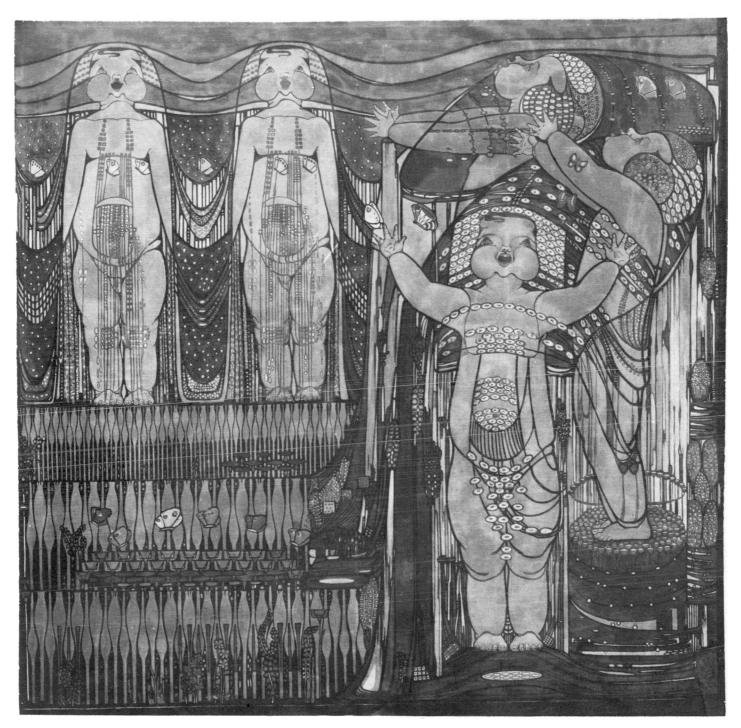

According to Mrs Mary Newbery Sturrock these two panels were painted by Margaret and are inspired by the words of the 65th Psalm: 'Thou crownest the year with Thy goodness . . . and the little hills shall rejoice.' As with *The Opera of the Sea* Mackintosh seems to have used motifs from the panels in his textile designs. The extent of this use, however, and its variety, suggests that Mackintosh may have contributed to the detailed design of the panels, although they were apparently painted solely by Margaret

Blk) Design for Chiffon-voile with different arrangement of color-scheme

Margaret Macdonald Mackintosh
2 Cedar Studios
44a. Glebe Place Chelsea S.W.3.

53 Margaret Macdonald
    Mackintosh Stylised
    roses – chiffon voile
    *Pentil and watercolour on
    tracing paper 250 × 200*
    Private collection

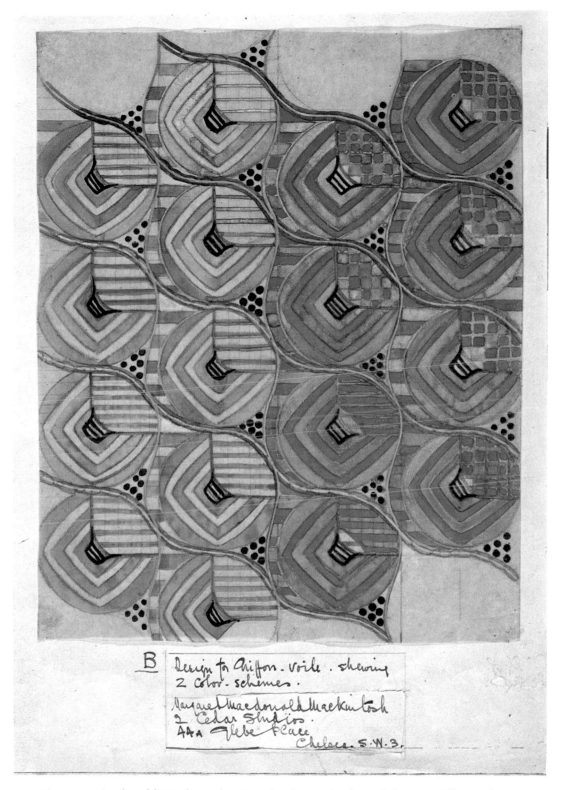

B Design for chiffon voile showing 2 colour schemes.

Margaret Macdonald Mackintosh
2 Cedar Studios.
44a Glebe Place
Chelsea. S.W.3.

54 Margaret Macdonald Mackintosh   Circles, lines, checks and dots – chiffon voile
Pencil and watercolour on tracing paper 251 × 200   Private collection

A more formalised and abstract development of No. 53 showing alternative colourways

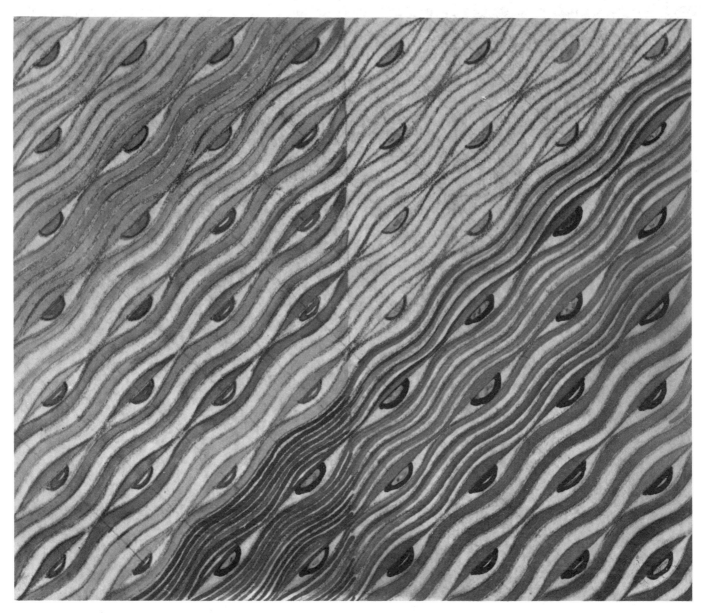

55 Margaret Macdonald Mackintosh   Wave pattern – voile   *Pencil and watercolour on tracing paper*
180 × 208   Glasgow University

Margaret has given the manufacturer a choice of colour and treatment in this design and also gives
instructions that it can be printed on the diagonal, horizontal or vertical

56 Saltire *Pencil and watercolour 199 × 259* Glasgow University

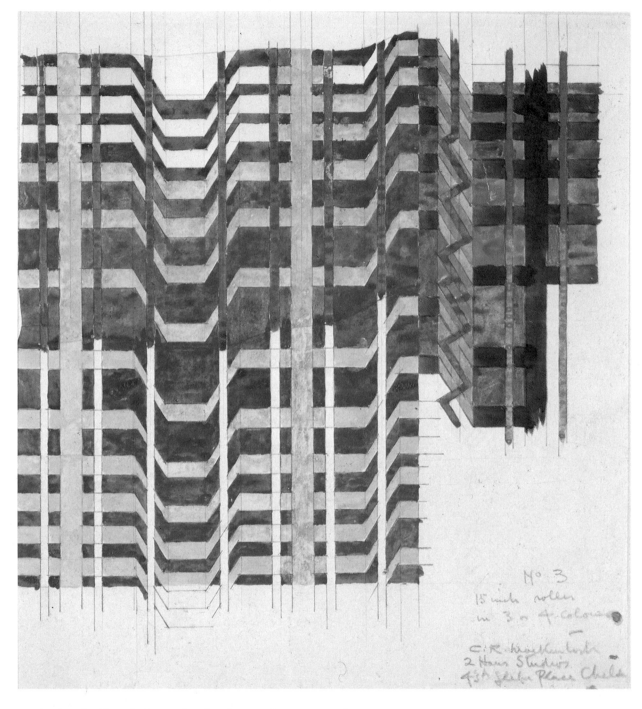

57 Red and yellow lattice   *Pencil and watercolour 525 × 428*
Glasgow University

One of the more architectural of the designs, using a rigid
geometric grid and bold colours. It was to be printed by a
15-inch roller in three or four colours

58 (*opposite*) Orange chevrons   *Pencil and watercolour 555 × 503*   Glasgow University

66

Various designs & Colour Schemes

E

59 Wave pattern – purple and black   *Pencil and watercolour 162 × 215*   Glasgow University

60 (*opposite*) Chequered rectangles   *Pencil and watercolour 169 × 140*   Victoria and Albert Museum

K

C. R. Mackintosh
2 Hans Studios
43A Glebe Place
Chelsea   S. W. 3

61 Stripes and checks – purple and
blue *Pencil and watercolour on tracing
paper 258 × 137* Glasgow University

This design was offered to Sefton's for
production

62 Stripes and checks – purple, blue and orange *Pencil and watercolour on tracing paper 180 × 110* Glasgow University

63 Waves and zigzag *Pencil and watercolour 232 × 178*
Glasgow University

A note on the mount indicates that this design was planned as a 15-inch
repeat in three colours. A similar drawing (collection: Glasgow
University) shows how the zigzag pattern evolved from stylised leaves

64   Purple triangles   *Pencil and watercolour 150 × 163*   Glasgow University

65   Furniture fabric – blue, black, purple and white   *Pencil and watercolour on tracing paper*
298 × 217   Glasgow University

Mackintosh described this design as a 'furniture fabric' – whether it was intended for
upholstered furniture, or for splash-backs of washstands, is not clear

66 Wave pattern – purple, pink, orange and black *Pencil and watercolour 492 × 378*
Glasgow University

A finished design with a repeat of 10 inches and giving an alternative colourway of
yellow, black and orange. The whiplash motif, seen here in white or orange checks,
appears in a number of other drawings

67 Printed shantung *Printed by William Foxton* c. *1919* Victoria and Albert Museum

68 Furnishing fabric – orange and black *Pencil and watercolour 237 × 176* Private collection

69 Waves – yellow, orange, blue and black   *Pencil and watercolour on tracing paper 265 × 220*
Glasgow University

The most abstract of any of Mackintosh's surviving designs, it owes nothing to the organic or
geometric origins of most of his other drawings

78

BIBLIOGRAPHY

Books

Alison, Filippo, *Charles Rennie Mackintosh as a Designer of Chairs*, London, 1974 (English edition of catalogue of an exhibition organised by Professor Alison for the Milan Triennale, 1973).

Billcliffe, Roger, *Mackintosh Watercolours*, London, 1978.

Billcliffe, Roger, *Charles Rennie Mackintosh: The Complete Furniture, Furniture Drawings and Interior Designs*, London, 1979; second edition, 1980.

Howarth, Thomas, *Charles Rennie Mackintosh and the Modern Movement*, London, 1952. Reprinted with new Introduction and enlarged Bibliography, 1977.

Macleod, Robert, *Charles Rennie Mackintosh*, London, 1968.

Pevsner, Nikolaus, *Studies in Art, Architecture and Design*, vol. II: *Victorian and After*, London, 1968 (includes translation of author's monograph on Mackintosh, first published in Milan, 1950).

Exhibition Catalogues

1933 *Charles Rennie Mackintosh, Margaret Macdonald Mackintosh: A Memorial Exhibition*. McLellan Galleries, Glasgow.

1953 *Charles Rennie Mackintosh*. An exhibition organised by Thomas Howarth for the Saltire Society, Edinburgh, and Arts Council of Great Britain.

1968 *Charles Rennie Mackintosh: Architecture, Design, Painting*. Centenary exhibition sponsored by the Edinburgh Festival Society and the Scottish Arts Council. Catalogue by Andrew McLaren Young. Also shown at the Victoria and Albert Museum, London; smaller versions of the exhibition travelled to Zurich, Vienna and Darmstadt.

1977 *Flower Drawings by Charles Rennie Mackintosh*. Hunterian Museum, University of Glasgow and The Fine Art Society, London. Catalogue by Roger Billcliffe.

1978 *Mackintosh Watercolours*. Glasgow Art Gallery and The Fine Art Society, Edinburgh and London. Catalogue by Roger Billcliffe.

1978 *Charles Rennie Mackintosh 1868–1928: A Memorial Tribute*. An exhibition of works from the collection of Thomas Howarth at the Art Gallery of Ontario, Toronto. Text by Thomas Howarth; catalogue by Maria Etkind and Katharine Jordan Lochnan.

1978 *Charles Rennie Mackintosh: The Chelsea Years 1915–1923*. Hunterian Museum, University of Glasgow. Catalogue by Pamela Reekie.

INDEX